HEALTH AND SAFETY

Joanne Suter

SADDLEBACK
EDUCATIONAL PUBLISHING

21st CENTURY
LIFESKILLS

Moving Out on Your Own
Everyday Household Tasks
Health and Safety
Managing Money
Consumer Spending
Job Search
Getting Ahead at Work
Community Resources
Transportation and Travel
Car and Driver

SADDLEBACK
EDUCATIONAL PUBLISHING
www.sdlback.com

ISBN: 978-1-61651-120-3
eBook: 978-1-60291-851-1

Printed in the U.S.A.

24 23 22 21 20   8 9 10 11 12

CONTENTS

UNIT [1]

PREVIEW | Prevention: The Best Cure

■ How much do you already know about the material in this unit? Circle letters or words to correctly complete the sentences. Answers are upside down at the bottom of the page.

1. *Hygiene* has to do with habits of (nutrition / cleanliness).

2. The *Food Pyramid* is a type of (supermarket display / dietary guide).

3. When you're cooking, keep pot handles turned toward the (front / back) of the stove.

4. Aerobic exercise increases the body's ability to (use oxygen / bear heavy weight).

5. It's best to exercise (occasionally / regularly).

6. Bone-building calcium can be found in (milk / peaches).

7. Experts recommend exercising
   a. once a week.
   b. three to seven times a week.
   c. two to three times a month.

8. To have healthy hair, you should **not**
   a. lend or borrow hats.
   b. use shampoo.
   c. brush your hair.

9. The largest portion of your daily diet should come from the food group containing
   a. sweets.
   b. protein.
   c. grains.

10. To put out a grease fire in the kitchen, use
    a. water.
    b. baking soda.
    c. coffee.

LESSON

1   Physical Fitness

Think about the challenges your body faced today. Did you run to the bus stop? Did you carry a heavy backpack? Did you play a sport? Your body's ability to meet daily demands is called *physical fitness*. Regular exercise is a key to physical fitness. It helps you stay healthy and look and feel your best.

Aerobic exercises strengthen your heart. During aerobic exercise, you breathe in more oxygen (air) and your body uses it in an effective way. Swimming, biking, and running are some examples of aerobic exercises. Although lifting weights builds muscle strength, it is not an aerobic activity. Aerobic exercise makes your heart beat faster. It pumps more blood to your muscles and provides them with more oxygen. Aerobic power helps you do hard, physical work. How much aerobic exercise is enough? Mayo Clinic says at least 30 minutes of daily aerobic activity can help you live a longer and healthier life.

Exercise is a *must* for good health—but be sure to exercise safely. Warm up first to loosen up your muscles

before you put them to work. Stretch before exercising to reduce chances of injury. After your activity, make sure to give your muscles time to cool down and relax.

Most people who exercise regularly say they couldn't get along without it! Scientists have found that the body releases special chemicals during exercise. These chemicals, called *endorphins*, create a sense of well-being and reduce feelings of stress.

Exercise helps you maintain proper weight by burning calories (units of food energy). The chart below shows how many calories are burned by different exercises. The numbers on the chart relate to someone who weighs 150 pounds. Calories are used at different rates, depending on a person's weight. If you weigh 75 pounds, you will use up half as many calories as a 150-pound person doing the same exercise for the same amount of time.

FOOD	CALORIES	MINUTES WALKING (4 MPH)	MINUTES OF HIGH-IMPACT AEROBICS	MINUTES JOGGING (5.2 MPH)
Chocolate chip muffin	364	67	44	34
1/4-lb. cheeseburger w/ bun	552	103	66	51
Pizza, meat & veggie, thick crust, one slice	233	43	28	22
The above calorie counts are from http://www.myfoodapedia.gov. Calorie burn times calculated at http://www.healthdiscovery.net/links/calculators/calorie_calculator.htm.				

■ Thinking It Over

1. Physical fitness is your
   a. body's ability to perform daily activities.
   b. skill level at a certain sport.
   c. appearance in stylish clothing.

2. One key to physical fitness is
   a. studying very hard.
   b. exercising regularly.
   c. eating a lot of calories.

3. Aerobic exercise builds
   a. good study skills.
   b. a healthy heart.
   c. layers of fat.

4. Aerobic exercise provides muscles with more
   a. calories.
   b. flexibility.
   c. oxygen.

■ Key Vocabulary

1. Exercise that causes you to breathe in more air and use it better is called _____.

2. *Endorphins* are chemicals that can reduce feelings of _____.

3. Food energy is measured in units called _____.

■ Everyday Math

Hector runs to school 5 days a week. It takes him 15 minutes to get there. (He rides the bus home.) He also swims laps in the community pool for 30 minutes every Saturday. According to Mayo Clinic's recommendation, does Hector get enough aerobic activity each week?

_____

■ Comparing

1. Which activity provides aerobic exercise—weight-lifting or running?

   _____

2. Which type of exercise is more vigorous—riding a bike less than 10 mile per hour or swimming?

   _____

3. Which activity could be called aerobic—lying down for a nap or taking a walk?

   _____

■ On Your Own

Most people walk somewhere during a usual day's activities. How could you make walking more aerobic?

_____

_____

_____

_____

LESSON

2   Hygiene

People look and feel better when they are clean. Good hygiene habits can put you on the road to good health and help protect you from germs. Evaluate your own hygiene by answering the questions below.

GERM-GUARDS: Do you . . .

YES NO

- regularly shower or bathe? ☐ ☐
- wash your hands often with soap and water? ☐ ☐
- wash the front and backs of your hands and between your fingers and thumbs? ☐ ☐
- wash your hands long enough? (to sing the Happy Birthday song twice) ☐ ☐
- dry your hands with a clean towel after washing? ☐ ☐
- cover your nose with a tissue whenever you sneeze, or sneeze into your upper sleeve? ☐ ☐
- cover your cough with a tissue or the back of your hand? ☐ ☐

HEALTHY HAIR: Do you . . .

- wash your hair regularly? ☐ ☐
- use an antidandruff shampoo if you have a flaky scalp? ☐ ☐
- follow the directions on your shampoo bottle? ☐ ☐
- regularly clean your combs, brushes, and pillowcases? ☐ ☐
- wear only your own hats and use only your own combs and brushes? ☐ ☐

DENTAL DEFENSE: Do you . . .

- clean your teeth after eating? ☐ ☐

- brush both the outside and inside surfaces of your teeth?

YES NO

☐ ☐
- brush your tongue to remove germs that can cause bad breath? ☐ ☐
- rinse your mouth well with water or mouthwash after brushing? ☐ ☐
- use dental floss at least once a day? ☐ ☐
- have regular dental check-ups? ☐ ☐
- eat a well-balanced diet? ☐ ☐
- avoid sugary food? ☐ ☐

ACNE ANNIHILATORS: Do you . . .

- drink plenty of water (at least eight glasses a day)? ☐ ☐
- wash your face at least twice a day (morning and night)? ☐ ☐
- wash your face after physical workouts? ☐ ☐
- know your own skin type (dry, oily, or combination) and use skin products that are right for you? ☐ ☐
- keep your hair clean and off your face? ☐ ☐
- avoid squeezing pimples? ☐ ☐
- consult a dermatologist about severe skin problems? ☐ ☐

How many questions did you answer with a *yes*? Your *yes* answers point to good hygiene habits.

■ **Thinking It Over:** Write **T** for *true* or **F** for *false.*

1. ____ Good hair hygiene means using only your own combs and brushes.

2. ____ Trading hats with friends may seem fun but it is not a healthful practice.

3. ____ The only time to see a dentist is when you have a toothache.

4. ____ The best way to get rid of a pimple is to squeeze it.

5. ____ Drinking lots of water may help cure your acne.

■ **Key Vocabulary**

1. *Hygiene* has to do with your
   a. habits of cleanliness.
   b. eating habits.
   c. exercise routines.

2. If you have a flaky scalp, you have
   a. acne.
   b. dandruff.
   c. hair loss.

3. If you have acne, you have
   a. pimples.
   b. dimples.
   c. dandruff.

4. To *annihilate* something means to
   a. purchase it.
   b. get rid of it.
   c. wear it often.

5. A *dermatologist* is a
   a. hair stylist.
   b. dental surgeon.
   c. skin specialist.

■ **Cause and Effect**

1. If you don't use a tissue when you sneeze, _____

   _____.

2. Tooth decay can result from

   _____

   _____.

3. Forgetting to brush your tongue can cause you to have _____

   _____.

■ **On Your Own**

What one hygiene practice do you think you should change? How might you improve your habits?

   _____

   _____

   _____

   _____

   _____

LESSON

3 Nutrition

Eating nutritious, or healthful, foods is one important step you can take toward well-being. A balanced diet can help you feel fit and look good.

What is a "balanced" diet? To answer that question, the U.S. Department of Agriculture (USDA) developed the Food Pyramid. It recommends that people choose foods from the six major food groups. Notice that you should eat a greater daily amount from the groups in the *widest* sections of the pyramid. The foods in the *narrowest* sections should be eaten in the smallest amounts.

Discretionary Calories such as those from sweets, are not included in the pyramid because they are not considered *essentials*.

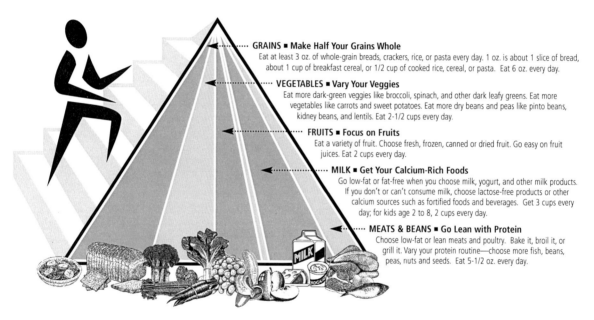

GRAINS ▪ Make Half Your Grains Whole
Eat at least 3 oz. of whole-grain breads, crackers, rice, or pasta every day. 1 oz. is about 1 slice of bread, about 1 cup of breakfast cereal, or 1/2 cup of cooked rice, cereal, or pasta. Eat 6 oz. every day.

VEGETABLES ▪ Vary Your Veggies
Eat more dark-green veggies like broccoli, spinach, and other dark leafy greens. Eat more vegetables like carrots and sweet potatoes. Eat more dry beans and peas like pinto beans, kidney beans, and lentils. Eat 2-1/2 cups every day.

FRUITS ▪ Focus on Fruits
Eat a variety of fruit. Choose fresh, frozen, canned or dried fruit. Go easy on fruit juices. Eat 2 cups every day.

MILK ▪ Get Your Calcium-Rich Foods
Go low-fat or fat-free when you choose milk, yogurt, and other milk products. If you don't or can't consume milk, choose lactose-free products or other calcium sources such as fortified foods and beverages. Get 3 cups every day; for kids age 2 to 8, 2 cups every day.

MEATS & BEANS ▪ Go Lean with Protein
Choose low-fat or lean meats and poultry. Bake it, broil it, or grill it. Vary your protein routine—choose more fish, beans, peas, nuts and seeds. Eat 5-1/2 oz. every day.

The U.S. Food and Drug Administration (FDA) requires that food companies live up to their claims. You can be sure of what you're getting when you see these words on product labels.

free (as in sugar-*free*): Product contains none, or almost none, of the ingredient.

fresh (as in *fresh* grapefruit juice): Product is raw and has not been heated or frozen.

high (as in *high* in fiber): Product provides 20 percent or more of the Daily Value (DV) of the nutrient per serving.

light or **lite** (as in *lite* cream cheese): Product must signal how it is improved relative to the traditional food. For example, it may contain one-third fewer calories, or one-half the fat or sodium in the regular product.

good source of (as in *good source of* calcium): A serving of the product provides 10 to 19 percent of the Daily Value of the nutrient named.

Thinking It Over

1. The Food Pyramid advises you to eat a *greater* daily amount from the

   a. meats and beans group.

   b. fruits group.

   c. grains group.

2. The Food Pyramid recommends that you eat the *lesser* daily amount from the

   a. milk group.

   b. oils group.

   c. vegetables group.

3. If you're looking for calcium, you'll find it in foods within the

   a. grains group.

   b. oils group.

   c. milk group.

4. A *vegetarian* (person who chooses not to eat meat) can get necessary protein from

   a. rice.

   b. beans.

   c. candy.

Everyday Math

For lunch, Diego ate a peanut butter sandwich (2 slices of bread, 2 tablespoons or 1 ounce of peanut butter).

1. How many ounces/ounce equivalents from the grains group did Diego's lunch provide?

   _____

2. How many ounces/ounce equivalents from the meats and beans group does Diego have left to consume for the day?

   _____

Key Vocabulary: Abbreviations

1. The abbreviation *USDA* stands for the _____

   _____.

2. In a recipe, the abbreviation *tbsp.* stands for _____.

3. The *FDA* is the _____

   _____.

4. The abbreviation for *Daily Value* is _____.

Comparing

1. Foods from the wider sections on the pyramid should be eaten (more / less) often than foods in the narrower sections.

2. You should eat (more / less) meat than vegetables.

3. Milk contains (more / less) calcium than bread.

On Your Own

Choose one group from the pyramid. List foods from that group that you ate or will eat today.

_____

_____

_____

LESSON

4 Staying Safe at Home

What is the first thing you should buy to make your home safe? First take a guess, and then read on.

The answer is a rubber bath mat! More people are injured in the bathtub than in any other part of the house. A bath mat can prevent slips and falls. Home safety hint number one: Use a rubber bath mat!

This lesson will take you through Jake and Jen's house. These two really need some home safety hints! Most home accidents take place in the bathroom, in the kitchen, or on the stairs.

Jake is tired and wants to take a bath. He'll listen to some tunes at the same time. He plugs in his radio next to the tub and hops in the water. Hey, Jake can't hear the music! He reaches out to turn up the sound. . . .

Did you spot the trouble? Jake needs some safety hints:

• Never use hairdryers, radios (except shower radios), TVs, or any electrical appliances near water. Don't touch them when you're wet. Electricity and water don't mix. Together, they can kill!

• Check the water before you hop into the tub. You can get burned if the water is too hot.

Here are some more bathroom safety hints:

• Keep cleaning supplies and pills in a cupboard out of children's reach.

• Use childproof caps on pill bottles.

• Throw away pills that are old or are no longer used.

Now . . . on to the kitchen. See if you can spot danger there.

Jen is busy cooking. A pot is on the stove with its handle facing her. Now Jen spills a cup of milk onto the floor. She leaves it for the cat to lap up later. Next Jen takes raw meat off the cutting board and puts it in a pan. Then she slices a pear on the same board.

Jen's kitchen is full of safety hazards! She could use a few hints:

• First, turn all pot handles toward the back of the stove and away from other burners. Never point them to the front. It is too easy to knock them off the stovetop. Other burners can make pot handles too hot to touch, too.

• Don't wait to wipe up spills. Someone might slip on them.

• Raw meat can carry germs. Thoroughly clean anything that raw meat touches before putting it away or using it for something else.

Here are some more kitchen hints:

• To unplug equipment, always pull on the plug, not on the cord.

• Don't use water on a grease fire. Instead, put the fire out with baking soda. To be extra safe, keep a fire extinguisher nearby.

• Childproof all cupboards. The kitchen is full of utensils and cleaners that are dangerous to children and pets.

■ Thinking It Over

1. What is one safety hint for the bathroom?

   _____

   _____

2. What is one safety hint for the kitchen?

   _____

   _____

3. Most hints in the article would work in *both* the bathroom and kitchen. Name one hint that would be useful *only* in the kitchen.

   _____

   _____

■ Key Vocabulary

1. An _____ is an unplanned event that injures someone.

2. A tool that puts out flames by spraying a liquid or gas is called a fire _____.

3. Electrical _____ are machines and tools powered by electricity.

4. A dangerous condition in your home is called a safety _____.

■ Recalling Details

1. Using a rubber bath mat can keep you from _____ and _____.

2. Putting baking soda on a grease fire can _____.

3. Always turn pot handles _____ _____.

4. Always keep _____ and _____ _____ out of children's reach.

5. Never touch electrical appliances when _____ _____.

■ On Your Own

1. List two or more safety hints that are *not* mentioned in the article.

   _____

   _____

   _____

   _____

2. Describe one way you could make your own home safer.

   _____

   _____

   _____

   _____

UNIT [1]   REVIEW | Prevention: The Best Cure

A. Answer the questions to show what you know about the material you studied in this unit.

1. Tell one way that regular exercise helps your body. _____

_____

2. Name two items you can use to keep your teeth healthy.

_____   _____

3. List three foods that provide *protein*. _____

_____   _____

4. Name one item you should have near your bathtub and one item you should *not* have there. Explain your answers.

NEAR: _____

NOT NEAR: _____

B. Use key words from the unit to complete the sentences.

1. Your _____ pumps more blood when you exercise.

2. The FDA uses the _____ _____ diagram to illustrate a healthy diet.

3. Use _____ and water to make your hands germ-free.

4. You can reduce your risk of injury if you _____ before exercising.

5. To maintain good health, one to three to cups or cup equivalents of _____ each day.

6. More people are injured in the _____ than in any other part of the house.

C. Write three rules that would make *your* home safer.

1. _____

2. _____

3. _____

PREVIEW | Getting Medical Attention

UNIT [2]

■ How much do you already know about the material in this unit? Circle letters or words to correctly complete the sentences. Answers are upside down at the bottom of the page.

1. Health insurance protects people against (getting seriously sick / overwhelming medical costs).

2. A doctor who is highly trained in one field of medicine is called a (specialist / primary care provider).

3. People can often get medical insurance through their (workplace / supermarket).

4. A routine visit to the doctor usually includes a (hearing / blood pressure) check.

5. Dentists use anesthetics like novocaine to (block pain / prevent tooth decay).

6. Dentists most often treat a minor cavity by (filling / pulling) the tooth.

7. A dermatologist is a doctor who treats diseases of
   a. the eyes.
   b. the skin.
   c. childhood.

8. If you want to get your teeth straightened, you should visit an
   a. orthopedic surgeon.
   b. oral surgeon.
   c. orthodontist.

9. When you feel tense and stressed out, it often helps to:
   a. eat more bread.
   b. talk to someone.
   c. keep your troubles to yourself.

10. A good way to find a mental health therapist is through
   a. a school counselor.
   b. the Internet.
   c. the newspaper classified ads.

LESSON

1 Health Insurance

What is health insurance?

Health insurance protects people against the high costs of medical treatment. Health policies pay for portions of health care costs such as doctor visits, hospital stays, surgeries, and laboratory tests. Some policies pay for prescription medicines. To pay for insurance coverage, you pay premiums to the insurance company.

Two types of policies are most common today. One is fee-for-services coverage. This type of policy allows a person to use any doctor or hospital. A second type of policy is the managed care, or HMO, plan. With this plan, patients select one doctor to manage their care. Visits to other providers must be arranged by your primary care physician (PCP). The fee-for-services plan gives patients freedom of choice, but it costs more. The managed care plan costs less, but it limits your choice of doctors. It may, however, pay higher benefits.

Do you need health insurance?

Many young people don't think they need insurance. But they can get very sick and have accidents too—and they'll need health care. Most people can't handle the skyrocketing costs of health care without insurance. Study the following chart of sample U.S. treatment prices. Ask yourself, "Could I pay for that treatment out of my pocket? Do I need health insurance?"

MEDICAL PROCEDURE	SAMPLE COST OF TREATMENT
stitches for deep wound	$691
CT scan of head/brain	$2,090
appendectomy (operation to remove infected appendix)	$15,850 (2-day hospital stay)

Where do you get health insurance?

Most people purchase group insurance through their work. Employers offer certain plans and pay part or all of the premiums. If you cannot get health insurance through an employer, you may need to buy an individual plan. Group insurance is generally less costly than individual plans.

Do you understand health insurance?

When you enroll in a health insurance plan, you deal with special words. To understand your coverage, you must understand the vocabulary.

HEALTH INSURANCE GLOSSARY

benefit the amount of money paid to a medical provider

claim a request for payment under the terms of a policy

co-pay a set (typically small) amount an insured person pays for various drugs or services such a doctors visits, usually after the deductible is met

deductible the yearly amount *you* must pay before your insurer begins to pay the bills

exclusions conditions or treatments for which the insurer will *not* pay

HMO (Health Maintenance Organization) a group plan that requires your care be managed by one doctor; you choose that doctor from the insurer's list

preexisting condition a health problem you had *before* you applied for insurance; there may be a waiting period before treatments for such conditions are covered

premium the monthly amount of money you or your employer pays for insurance coverage

■ Thinking It Over

1. Health insurance helps you
   a. fight off colds and other viruses.
   b. pay health-care costs.
   c. receive wages when you're too sick to work.
2. Health insurance usually covers
   a. doctor's visits.
   b. hospital stays.
   c. both *a* and *b*.
3. The term *managed care* means
   a. one doctor oversees all your health services.
   b. you choose all your doctors and the services you receive.
   c. you do not have any health insurance.
4. Most people get their health insurance
   a. at the supermarket.
   b. after they are 80 years old.
   c. through their employer.

■ Everyday Math

Selena's health insurance pays 100 percent of all costs after Selena meets a $100 *deductible*. Selena broke her finger. The medical costs came to $250. This was Selena's first claim of the year.

1. How much did Selena have to pay? _____
2. How much did her health insurance pay? _____

■ Key Vocabulary

1. The written document that explains your health-care coverage is called your insurance _____ .
2. The amount of money you must pay each year before your insurance begins covering costs is called the _____ .
3. An insurance _____ is a request that the insurance company pay a bill.
4. _____ are the monthly payments made for health insurance coverage.

■ On Your Own

1. Would you be more likely to choose a *fee-for-services* or a *managed care* health plan? Give reasons for your answer.

   _____
   _____
   _____

2. Instead of buying health insurance, some people count on their savings to pay for health care. Do you think that's a good idea? Why or why not?

   _____
   _____
   _____

LESSON

2 The Doctor's Office

Sarah has had a sore throat for five days. She knows that when a health problem persists, it's time to call the doctor.

Dr. Miller's scheduling desk takes Sarah's call. Sarah says that she is ill and not seeking just a routine check-up. The scheduler gives Sarah a 3 o'clock appointment that day.

Sarah arrives at the office at a quarter to three. She'll use the 15 extra minutes to update her insurance information and fill out forms.

A nurse escorts Sarah to the examining room. The nurse follows the usual routine. She weighs Sarah and checks her blood pressure, pulse rate, and temperature. She records the information on Sarah's chart.

Alone in the examining room, Sarah checks her notes. She has come prepared. Keeping a patient healthy is not just the doctor's job. The patient has responsibilities, too. Doctors need information from the patient to make the right diagnosis and prescribe proper treatment.

Soon Dr. Miller comes in. She is a general practitioner. She works with the whole body and oversees regular medical care. Sometimes, if problems are very specific or severe, Dr. Miller sends a patient to a specialist. If Sarah's throat doesn't get better, Dr. Miller will make a referral to an ear, nose, and throat specialist.

First, Dr. Miller reviews Sarah's chart. Then she conducts a complete examination. Next, a technician draws some blood. When lab tests show that Sarah has an infection, Dr. Miller prescribes an antibiotic.

"We'll recheck your throat in 10 days," Dr. Miller says. "Please make an appointment on your way out."

WHAT IS BLOOD PRESSURE?

Blood pressure is the force of your blood against the artery walls. Your blood pressure can tell a doctor about the strength of your heart, the ease of blood flow, and the health of your arteries.

HOW SHOULD YOU PREPARE FOR A DOCTOR'S VISIT?

- Make a "problem list." Write down specific symptoms.

- Note any allergies or side effects you've had from medications. Tell your doctor about them.

- Write down questions. Feel free to check your notes while you're talking to the doctor.

DO YOU KNOW WHAT THESE SPECIALISTS TREAT?

pediatrician: babies and children

dermatologist: diseases of the skin

ophthalmologist: diseases of the eye

orthopedic surgeon: injured or diseased bones and joints

■ Thinking It Over

1. You should call your doctor
   a. whenever you feel unwell.
   b. when a health problem does not improve.
   c. at least once a month.

2. A doctor's office visit usually includes a check of your
   a. teeth, gums, and breath.
   b. sleeping habits.
   c. weight, pulse, and blood pressure.

3. Before a doctor's visit, it's a good idea to
   a. talk to a friend about the visit.
   b. make notes and write down questions.
   c. eat a healthy meal and take a nap.

4. A *general practitioner* is a doctor who
   a. handles routine health care.
   b. specializes in treating one part of the body.
   c. has not been practicing medicine for long.

■ Key Vocabulary

1. Blood vessels that carry blood from the heart throughout the body are called

   _____ .

2. When doctors give a

   _____ ,

   they send their patient to another health care provider.

3. A doctor who treats a specific type of problem is called a

   _____ .

4. _____ are medicines that kill or stop the growth of germs.

■ Putting Details in Order: Write numbers to put the activities in the correct order.

_____ get a doctor's prescription

_____ schedule a follow-up appointment

_____ call a doctor's office for an appointment

_____ have a check of blood pressure

_____ have a doctor's examination

■ On Your Own

Name two medical specialists *not* mentioned in the article. Explain what each specialist does.

_____

_____

_____

_____

_____

_____

LESSON

3 Dental Treatment

Bite! Chew! Talk! Smile! Your teeth get a big workout every day. You, your dentist, and the dental office staff make up the team that keeps your teeth and gums strong and healthy. Most dental problems can be prevented with the proper care.

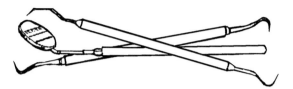

may sometimes need to pull, or extract, a tooth.

PREVENTATIVE CARE: Experts suggest dental check-ups twice a year. A regular visit is likely to include:

- instructions on oral hygiene (tooth brushing and flossing)
- oral prophylaxis (technical words for routine teeth cleaning)
- treatments to discourage tooth decay (cavities) such as fluoride and tooth sealant (a plastic material bonded over grooves in the teeth)
- an examination of teeth and gums
- X-rays to check for hidden cavities

EMERGENCY CARE: Most dentists will see emergency cases right away. If your own dentist is not available, the office can usually refer you elsewhere for emergency care. You should consider it a dental emergency if you have:

- severe pain or bleeding
- an injury to your teeth

RESTORATIVE SERVICES: Dentists usually repair damage done by tooth decay with fillings. Cavities may be filled with metal, porcelain, or gold.

ORAL SURGERY: Dentists (either your regular dentist or an oral surgeon)

ORTHODONTIC SERVICES: Straight, evenly spaced teeth create a great smile. They also help a person bite and chew correctly. An *orthodontist* is a dentist who specializes in straightening crooked teeth.

COSMETIC TREATMENTS: Some dental treatments are solely meant to improve appearance. Teeth bleaching or "whitening" has become a popular cosmetic service. Dentists may also use porcelain to hide dental imperfections.

PAIN CONTROL: Thanks to skilled dentists and local anesthetics like novocaine, modern treatments are usually pain-free. Procedures that are likely to be uncomfortable may be done under a general anesthetic, which puts the patient to sleep.

WHY SEE A DENTIST?

- repair tooth decay
- make your teeth look whiter
- get rid of bad breath (halitosis)
- straighten crooked teeth
- learn proper brushing technique
- remove plaque—a sticky, bacteria-filled substance that causes cavities

---

■ **Thinking It Over:** Write **T** for *true* or **F** for *false*.

1. _____ You need to see a dentist only when you have a toothache.

2. _____ Teeth cleaning is part of a routine dental visit.

3. _____ Dentists often provide tooth care education.

4. _____ Dentists take care of your gums as well as your teeth.

5. _____ The most common treatment for a cavity is pulling the tooth.

6. _____ Cement is the material dentists most often use for fillings.

7. _____ Dentists sometimes bleach teeth to make them whiter.

8. _____ Bleaching teeth can prevent tooth decay.

9. _____ A lack of regular dental care can cause bad breath.

■ **Everyday Math**

About how long should a person go between routine dental visits?

_____

■ **Key Vocabulary**

1. An *anesthetic* is a drug used to dull the sense of (feeling / hearing).

2. An *orthodontist* is a dentist who specializes in (straightening teeth / pain-free treatment).

3. Treatments that are meant only to improve appearance are called (*cosmetic* / *restorative*).

4. (*Fluoride* / *novocaine*) is used to discourage tooth decay.

■ **Recalling Details**

1. Which of the following would be considered a dental emergency?

   a. yellow teeth

   b. a broken tooth

   c. crooked teeth

2. Which substance do dentists use to block pain?

   a. tooth sealant

   b. porcelain

   c. novocaine

3. Why do dentists take X-rays?

   a. to reduce pain

   b. to find cavities

   c. to clean teeth

■ **On Your Own**

How could you persuade someone to get a dental check-up? Give at least three reasons.

_____

_____

_____

_____

_____

LESSON

4 Mental Health

Everyone gets the blues and the blahs now and then! We all face mental stress and strain. So, how do we deal with unpleasant emotions when life gets tough?

HELPING YOURSELF

Breathe deeply. People in a hurry or under stress tend to take shallow breaths. So when you feel tense, take a deep breath. Fill your lungs, count to four, and then let out the breath.

Keep active and fit. Exercise can melt away stress, so go for a run or shoot some hoops. Eat well and get plenty of rest. Creative activities—including dancing, painting, or singing—can relax your mind and lift your spirit too.

Reach for a security blanket. Did you once drag around an old blanket? Special items can make us feel safe when facing stress and tension. Wearing "lucky" sneakers might calm an athlete's nerves. Carrying a special coin might settle an actor's stage fright. What makes you feel safe and secure?

CONFIDING IN FRIENDS

Talk about it! Just putting a problem into words can make you feel less anxious. There are different ways to get your troubles off your chest. If you're uncomfortable talking to someone about your problems, try writing them in a journal. When stress gets really hard to handle, go to someone you trust. It might be a parent, a favorite teacher, or an older brother or sister who lends you advice and support.

SEEKING PROFESSIONAL HELP

There may be times when you need to share your feelings with a professional. A mental health counselor or therapist is trained to help people sort through their problems. At therapy sessions, a professional may meet with you one-on-one, with your family, or with others who face similar situations. In the group, you'll get a chance to express your emotions. You'll learn more about your strengths and weaknesses. You'll get help with stopping unwanted behavior and communicating your feelings more clearly.

How do you find a good therapist or counselor? When you're looking for a therapist, ask people you trust to recommend someone. You might ask family members, religious leaders, or your family doctor. You can find help at school by talking to a trusted teacher or school guidance counselor. You can contact local mental health centers. The first therapist you see might not be right for you. If that happens, keep looking! Counselors and therapists have different personalities and different styles. To get the very best support and guidance, you'll need to find the right match for *you*.

■ Thinking It Over

1. To reduce stress, try (holding your breath / breathing deeply).

2. Exercise tends to (reduce / increase) stress.

3. It's a healthy practice to (talk about your problems / keep your troubles to yourself).

4. Having a "lucky" charm that makes you feel comfortable is (childish / common).

■ Recalling Details

1. If you don't feel comfortable talking about your problems, you might _____ about them.

2. Three sources of information about mental health therapy are _____ _____.

■ Key Vocabulary: Use the first letter as a clue to the answer word.

1. Another word for *feelings* is
   e _____.

2. A mental health counselor who helps people deal with stressful problems may also be called a
   t _____.

3. Another word for *diary* is
   j _____.

■ Idioms

1. The expression "gets the blues" means

   a. feels sad.

   b. becomes angry.

   c. feels sick.

2. A "security blanket" is

   a. a cover that keeps you warm.

   b. an item that calms you and makes you feel safe.

   c. a locked safe or box.

3. To "get your troubles off your chest" is to

   a. take off a sweater or coat that is too heavy or warm.

   b. express your feelings rather than keeping them to yourself.

   c. make your problems worse by involving others in them.

■ On Your Own

Who do you talk to when you feel the need to "get something off your chest"? Why is he or she a good person to turn to?

_____

_____

_____

_____

_____

_____

UNIT [2] REVIEW | Getting Medical Attention

A. Answer the questions to show what you know about the material you studied in this unit.

1. Name three things that a typical health insurance policy covers.

   _____

   _____

2. Name one thing you should do to prepare for a visit to the doctor's office.

   _____

3. Explain the advantages and disadvantages of two types of health insurance.

   _____

   _____

   _____

4. List three things a patient can expect to happen during a routine visit to a doctor's office.

   _____

   _____

   _____

B. Use key words from the unit to complete the sentences.

1. A _____ specializes in the care of children.

2. An _____ specializes in straightening crooked teeth.

3. When you feel overwhelmed by _____ , talk to someone you can trust.

4. An _____ is a dental test to look for hidden cavities.

C. Suppose you feel nervous and fearful about the way your life is going. List two ways you can help yourself and one way someone else might be able to help you.

1. _____

2. _____

3. _____

UNIT [3]

PREVIEW | Handling Health Problems

■ How much do you already know about the material in this unit? Circle letters or words to correctly complete the sentences. Answers are upside down at the bottom of the page.

1. Symptoms are your body's (warning signals / major organs).

2. Pain and fever in one region of your body can signal (depression / infection).

3. In most places, the number to call in a medical emergency is (0 / 9-1-1).

4. The abbreviation ER means a hospital's (emergency room / entrance rules).

5. If you suspect someone has been poisoned, you should (call for emergency medical services / buy an over-the-counter medicine).

6. A prescription medicine (requires a doctor's order / can be purchased off the supermarket shelf).

7. A *pharmacist* is a person trained to
   a. give first aid.
   b. prepare and sell medicines.
   c. do routine physical exams.

8. A medication *dosage* is
   a. the date the medicine should be thrown away.
   b. the name of the medicine.
   c. the amount of medicine to take at one time.

9. One way to save money when purchasing medicines is to
   a. use a friend's leftover prescription medicine.
   b. purchase a generic brand.
   c. use up old medicine that has been in the cabinet for several years.

10. The letters *Rx* stand for
    a. poison!
    b. prescription.
    c. registered nurse.

Answers: 1. warning signals 2. infection 3. 9-1-1 4. emergency room 5. call for emergency medical services 6. requires a doctor's order 7. b 8. c 9. b 10. b

LESSON

1   Recognizing Warning Signs

When a car's warning light comes on, it tells you that something is wrong. In the same way, your body uses warning signs such as pain or fever to signal trouble. It's important to pay attention to what your body tells you. Become familiar with the warning signs, or symptoms, of some common health problems. If you notice them, get help.

GENERAL WARNING SIGNS

The following symptoms warn that something may be wrong with your body. Don't ignore them! If they continue, seek medical advice.

- aches and pains
- fever, especially over 101°F (98.6°F–99.6°F is normal)
- coughing
- sneezing
- unexplainable weight gain or loss
- sores that don't heal
- rash
- feeling "strange" or unusual
- dizziness
- sleep problems
- feeling tired

The chart below alerts you to symptoms of common health problems that require treatment.

allergy
- frequent runny nose
- itchy, watery eyes
- symptoms occur during certain seasons
- antibiotics do not help symptoms

bacterial infection
- fever
- pain
- only a single problem region
- antibiotics help symptoms
- cough with rust colored or green mucus

depression (mental illness)
- continual sadness
- trouble sleeping or sleeping too much
- frequent, uncontrollable anger
- appetite changes
- feelings of hopelessness
- difficulty completing tasks
- lack of enjoyment of friends, activities

skin cancer
- change in size, color, shape, or border of a mole
- a mole of varied colors, especially red, white, or blue
- sores that don't heal

Thinking It Over

1. You should definitely call a doctor if your temperature is
   a. 98°.
   b. over 101°.
   c. 99°.

2. Antibiotics are most likely to help fight
   a. an infection.
   b. an allergy.
   c. depression.

3. A warning sign of skin cancer is a
   a. fever.
   b. cough.
   c. change in the shape of a mole.

4. If warning signs continue, you should
   a. seek medical help.
   b. read a self-help book.
   c. talk to a friend.

Everyday Math

When Marco took his temperature, the thermometer read 100.6°F.

1. Is Marco's temperature above or below normal? _____

2. Does Marco have a fever? _____

3. How many degrees will Marco's temperature need to drop before it can be called normal? _____

Key Vocabulary: Write **T** for *true* or **F** for *false*.

1. _____ A *symptom* is a sign that something may be wrong with your body.

2. _____ A *fever* is a body temperature below normal.

3. _____ *Depression* is a mental illness that causes feelings of sadness.

4. _____ A *mole* is a type of cough that doesn't go away.

5. _____ A *rash* is a pattern of unusual spots or colors on the skin.

Compare and Contrast

What is one difference in symptoms between an *allergy* and an *infection*?

_____

_____

_____

On Your Own

Think about the last time you had a cold, the flu, an infection, or an allergy problem. Name the health problem. Then list symptoms that signaled you were ill.

_____

_____

_____

_____

_____

LESSON 2

Quick Action: First Aid and the Emergency Room

Kim took a first aid class through the American Red Cross. She learned how to treat common problems such as insect bites, small cuts, minor muscle strains, and bruises. Kim also learned how to recognize an emergency and where to seek help. Listed below are symptoms that signal a medical emergency.

MEDICAL EMERGENCIES—CALL FOR HELP!

- Large or deep wound or burn
- Severe facial head, neck, or back injuries
- Bleeding that won't stop
- Continuous vomiting or diarrhea
- Sudden, severe, or continuing pain, especially headache
- Choking
- Very high fever
- Blacking out, losing consciousness
- Extreme behavior change, such as confusion
- Seizures (uncontrolled body movements)
- Extreme chest pain
- Evidence of poisoning (even without physical symptoms)

If Kim sees someone with any of these signs, she will dial emergency medical services (EMS). In most places, that number is 9-1-1. She'll be ready to give her name and phone number. She'll tell her exact location—the address, apartment number, closest cross street, and nearby landmarks. She will answer all questions. Kim will not hang up the phone until she is told to, and she will follow all instructions.

Sometimes a medical condition seems urgent but not immediately life-threatening. In these cases, Kim may take the patient in for medical aid herself. For example, a sprained ankle or a deep cut that doesn't spurt blood calls for a medical visit rather than an emergency call. If it is after hours, or if the doctor is not available, Kim can head to a hospital emergency room (ER). ER visits are expensive, and waits for medical attention can be long. That's why Kim's first choice will be an appointment with the regular doctor.

■ Thinking It Over

1. Which of the following does *not* signal a medical emergency?

   a. limping

   b. choking

   c. blacking out

2. Which of the following is a sign of a medical emergency?

   a. an itchy rash

   b. sneezing

   c. uncontrollable bleeding

3. Which is the usual telephone number for emergency aid?

   a. 0   b. 9-1-1   c. 555-1212

4. According to the reading, which agency offers first aid classes?

   a. American Red Cross

   b. The Peace Corps

   c. Meals on Wheels

5. If a medical condition appears to be immediately life-threatening, what should you do?

   a. Telephone for emergency medical services.

   b. Go to the emergency room.

   c. Run to a neighbor for help.

■ Abbreviations: What do the following abbreviations stand for?

1. EMS = _____

2. ER = _____

■ Key Vocabulary

_____ are uncontrolled body movements caused by a loss of muscle control.

■ Recalling Details: Give two reasons why you should choose a regular doctor visit over an emergency room visit, if possible.

● _____

_____

● _____

_____

■ Making Judgments: Write **FA** if you would give *first aid,* **9-1-1** if you would call for emergency help, or **ER** if you would go to the *emergency room.*

1. _____ mosquito bite

2. _____ small burn from a hot pan

3. _____ chest pain and blacking out

4. _____ swollen, painful ankle that may be sprained or broken

5. _____ continuous vomiting and empty bottle of pills

■ On Your Own

Does your family have a first aid kit? If so, list three items in it. If not, list three items that you think should be in a first aid kit.

_____

_____

_____

LESSON

3   Prescription Medicines

When Eric had an ear infection, his doctor prescribed a medicine to fight the infection. The doctor filled out a prescription form and gave it to Eric to take to the pharmacy. (In some cases, a doctor's office will phone the prescription in to the pharmacy that the patient chooses.) The form listed the name of the medication and the proper dosage. It told how many times Eric could refill the prescription. On the way to the pharmacy, Eric saw his friend Jasper. Eric showed Jasper the prescription.

"I have some of that medicine at home," said Jasper. "You can have mine!"

"No," Eric answered. "I'll get my own." Eric had heard that it is unwise to share prescription drugs. Sharing medicines can lead to dangerous drug interactions, wrong dosages, and allergic reactions, among other things.

Eric took his prescription to Fred's Friendly Pharmacy.

"Will you accept a generic brand of this drug?" the pharmacist asked. He explained that a less-familiar brand may be cheaper than the most well-known brand. He assured Eric that the medicine was the same.

In a few minutes the pharmacist called Eric to the counter. His prescription was ready. Since Eric had not used the drug before, the pharmacist explained side effects, or problems, the drug could cause.

"If you become sleepy, dizzy, or have a dry mouth, check with your doctor," the pharmacist warned.

Then he explained the bottle labeling to Eric. The label looked like the illustration below.

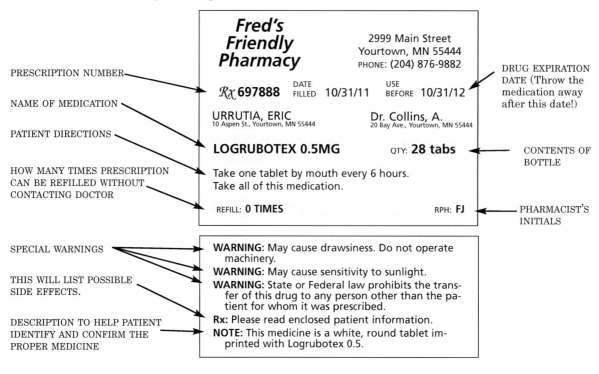

■ **Thinking It Over:** Write **T** for *true* or **F** for *false*.

1. _____ A prescription drug can be purchased without a doctor's order.

2. _____ A doctor may write a prescription or call it in to the pharmacy.

3. _____ It's a good idea to try out a friend's medicine before purchasing your own.

4. _____ The Rx number is the prescription number.

5. _____ The label on the bottle describes the medicine inside.

■ **Key Vocabulary**

1. A _____ is a doctor's instructions telling what medicine is to be prepared and how it should be taken.

2. The amount of medicine to be taken at one time is the

   _____.

3. Problems caused by a medicine are called _____ _____.

4. The _____ date is the time when the medicine should no longer be used.

5. A _____ is a person trained and licensed to prepare and sell prescription drugs.

6. The place where prescription drugs are prepared and sold is called a _____.

7. A _____ medicine does not have a well-known brand name.

■ **Everyday Math:** Study the label on page 30.

1. How many pills will the patient take in a 24-hour period?

   a. 4   b. 10   c. 2

2. How many days will this bottle of 28 tablets last?

   a. 14   b. 7   c. 28

3. The patient stops the medicine after taking how many tablets?

   a. all 28

   b. 14 (half the bottle)

   c. whenever the patient feels better

■ **On Your Own**

What are three things you would check before starting to take a new prescription drug?

_____

_____

_____

_____

31

LESSON

4   Over-the-Counter Medicines

You can find hundreds of over-the-counter (OTC) medicines on your local supermarket or drugstore shelves. These products compete for your attention and dollars. Read the labels carefully. When you don't know which choice is best, ask the store's pharmacist.

Read the chart below. It lists some of the OTC products you may have in your home medicine cabinet.

PRODUCT	PURPOSE	COMMON CHOICES
antiseptic cleansers	to clean minor wounds	hydrogen peroxide, iodine, baking soda
pain and fever medications	to relieve pain, lower fever	aspirin, acetaminophen, ibuprofen
antacids	to relieve upset stomach	liquids, chewable pills, tablets
cold remedies	to treat runny nose, cough, and other cold symptoms	decongestants, antihistamines, nose drops, cough syrups, cold tablets
sunscreens	to prevent sunburn	lotions, creams, sprays

When buying, storing, and using OTC medicines, the following rules apply:

- Always read the product labels. Talk to your doctor or pharmacist if you have questions.

- Remember that over time, medications can go bad. Check the expiration dates on products in your medicine cabinet. As a rule of thumb, replace them at least every three years.

- Keep all drugs out of children's reach. No bottle is totally childproof!

- All drugs can cause side effects, such as drowsiness. Read labels carefully so you know what to expect.

- Don't assume that a drug is safe just because it doesn't require a prescription. Follow directions carefully to avoid dangerous problems. Avoid taking too little or too much.

- Pay attention to all warnings! Some OTC medicines can cause problems if they're taken along with certain prescription medicines. Not all medicines are safe for everyone! Conditions such as pregnancy or heart ailments may make the drug dangerous to you.

- You'll find different brands of most OTC medicines on store shelves. An expensive, well-advertised drug is not necessarily better than a less costly, generic one. As always, when you're in doubt, ask the pharmacist for advice.

■ Thinking It Over

1. You'd be likely to use hydrogen peroxide to

   a. stop a cough.

   b. prevent sunburn.

   c. clean a wound.

2. You should replace items in your medicine cabinet at least

   a. every three years.

   b. every year.

   c. whenever you move.

3. If you reach for an antacid, you probably have

   a. an upset stomach.

   b. a summer cold.

   c. a nasty cut.

4. When you have questions about over-the-counter (OTC) medicines, you should consult a

   a. dictionary.

   b. doctor or pharmacist.

   c. friend or relative.

■ Making Comparisons

1. How is an OTC medicine different from a prescription medicine?

   _____

   _____

2. What is one way OTC medicines and prescription medicines are alike?

   _____

   _____

■ Informal Language

What three-word phrase in the reading means "a general guideline to go by"?

_____

■ On Your Own

Find an OTC drug in your medicine chest. Study the package. Then answer the following questions:

1. What is the name of this medicine?

   _____

2. What is its purpose?

   _____

   _____

3. What is the proper dosage for a person your age?

   _____

   _____

4. What is one side effect that can occur with this medicine?

   _____

5. Are there any warnings on the label? If so, describe one.

   _____

   _____

   _____

6. What is the product expiration date?

   _____

UNIT [3]

right
right
right
HEALTH AND SAFETY

REVIEW | Handling Health Problems

A. Answer the questions to show what you know about the material you studied in this unit.

1. Name two symptoms that signal a medical emergency requiring immediate help.

   _____   _____

2. List two types of information you would find on the label of a prescription medicine.

   _____   _____

3. What should you do? Make a decision based on what you've read in this unit. Explain your decision.

   • *You have painful neck glands, a cough with green mucus, and a slight fever.*

   _____

   • *A friend suggests you try her prescription allergy medicine for your sneezing and itchy eyes.*

   _____

   • *You notice that a mole on your arm has changed shape, size, and color.*

   _____

B. Use words from the unit to complete the sentences.

1. An _____ may cause you to have itchy, watery eyes.
2. A _____ is the written form of a doctor's order for a certain medicine.
3. A _____ is a person who prepares and sells medicines.
4. Unintended reactions to medicines are called _____
   _____.

C. Why is it important to read medicine labels carefully? Write three reasons.

1. _____
2. _____
3. _____

34

UNIT [4]

PREVIEW | Avoiding Health Hazards

■ How much do you already know about the material in this unit? Circle letters or words to correctly complete the sentences. Answers are upside down at the bottom of the page.

1. *Peer pressure* is the influence of (friends / advertising).

2. (Nicotine / Alcohol) is found in tobacco.

3. Nonsmokers generally have (more / fewer) colds and coughs than smokers do.

4. The number one cause of auto accidents is (tobacco / alcohol) use.

5. Alcoholism is a (disease / treatment program) that involves problem drinking.

6. The HIV virus can be spread by contact with an infected person's (body fluids / skin).

7. Which is an example of resisting peer pressure?

   a. skipping classes because your friends are doing it

   b. saying no when offered a cigarette

   c. getting an A on a test

8. About what percentage of smokers say they'd like to quit?

   a. 5%

   b. 15%

   c. 80%

9. Why is it hard to quit smoking?

   a. Nicotine is habit-forming.

   b. Smoking makes you feel healthier.

   c. Smoking helps you do better in school or on the job.

10. A mother can damage her unborn baby if she does which of the following?

    a. drinks alcohol

    b. smokes tobacco

    c. both *a* and *b*

LESSON

1 Resisting Peer Pressure

It's great to have friends! Pals can be fun and can give you great advice. Sometimes, however, the best of friends can lead you down the wrong path. *Peer pressure*—being influenced or led by friends' advice and actions— can be a good thing sometimes. But in many cases it can be a negative thing.

First, let's look at the good kind of peer pressure. Cisco's friends are signing up for after-school activities. One joins a singing group. Another goes out for the volleyball team. Cisco doesn't want to be left out! He follows their lead and decides to get involved, too. This is a positive kind of peer pressure.

Then there's the negative kind of peer pressure. Say, for example, a lot of Sylvie's friends are getting tattoos. Actually, Sylvie thinks that body art is ugly. She's afraid of the health risks and worries how the markings will look 20 years from now. Her parents are also set against it! Still, Sylvie wants to fit in. Does she listen to her own feelings? Or does she do something that may have a negative effect on her health, body image, and her relations with her family?

In some situations, peer pressure can be *very* dangerous. These can be some of the hardest, but *most* important times to make a good choice. Deana's friend Rosa drives too fast and shows off behind the wheel. Some of her pals think it's funny—but Deana knows better. Does Deana cave in to peer pressure and get in the car with Rosa? Or does she assert herself, follow her better judgment, and stay safe?

Saying *no* to peers is certainly not easy. It may mean losing a friend, getting laughed at, or being left out. But the more often you stand up for your own beliefs, the easier it gets.

When you find yourself being drawn in by peer pressure, ask yourself these questions:

1. Am I risking my safety or health?

2. Could this activity hurt me or someone else?

3. Could I lose my parents' trust?

4. Is this something I really *want* to do?

Think for yourself. Even though "everyone" may be doing it—if something *feels* wrong, it probably is!

■ Thinking It Over

1. Peer pressure can lead a person to
    a. do good things.
    b. do bad things.
    c. both *a* and *b*.

2. The reading suggests that you should
    a. always take a friend's advice.
    b. follow your own beliefs.
    c. never make a friend angry.

3. According to the reading, saying *no* to peers is
    a. never a good idea.
    b. as easy as pie.
    c. usually difficult.

4. According to the reading, one way to feel comfortable standing up for yourself is to
    a. do it often.
    b. yell loudly.
    c. give up all your friends.

■ Key Vocabulary

1. Your _____ is a person who is your equal.

2. You _____ yourself when you speak out for what you believe and do what you think is best.

3. The opposite of *positive* is _____ .

4. _____ are designs made by injecting ink under the skin.

■ Informal Language

What two-word phrase in the reading is the opposite of *resist*? It means "to abandon your own ideas and give in to pressure."

_____

■ Summarizing

Write a sentence that sums up the main message of the reading.

_____

_____

_____

■ On Your Own

1. Think of three reasons it can be hard to say *no* to friends.

_____

_____

_____

2. Tell about a time you resisted peer pressure *or* about a time you followed the crowd.

_____

_____

_____

_____

_____

_____

LESSON

2 Tobacco

It's a well known fact that the nicotine in cigarettes and chewing tobacco is dangerous. Addiction to this habit-forming substance can destroy lives. Studies show that one in every five Americans will die from diseases caused by cigarettes and chewing tobacco.

No one says quitting tobacco is easy! Because nicotine is highly addictive, kicking the habit takes hard work and willpower. But those who stop using tobacco report many health benefits. They also save a lot of money. Tobacco is expensive!

It seems that many people are wising up. Studies show that the percentage of smokers is shrinking. Nearly 80 percent of all smokers say they'd like to quit, and about 65 percent have made more than one serious try. In one group, however, the number of cigarette smokers is on the rise. In many communities, more teenaged girls are smoking cigarettes.

But even some of those girls are quitting, too. Carrie was a teen smoker who can now say, "I quit!" She writes:

Smoking was my habit and hobby. Giving up smoking was like losing a friend. I needed to replace it. When I wanted to smoke, I did something else. I took a walk, went to the library, cleaned out a closet. Soon I was enjoying things I'd had trouble with before. I could run farther. I appreciated the smell of my own clean hair. Most of all, I felt powerful. I had taken control. I had beaten the habit.

SERIOUS HEALTH PROBLEMS RELATED TO TOBACCO USE:

- cancer
- stroke
- heart disease
- circulatory disease
- lung disease
- osteoporosis (bone loss)
- damage to unborn babies (caused by tobacco use during pregnancy)

NONSMOKERS USUALLY HAVE:

- more energy.
- more endurance.
- fewer coughs and colds.
- a better sense of smell and taste.

Ask yourself these questions:

	YES	NO		YES	NO
Does tobacco make me smarter?	❏	❏	Will tobacco use get me better grades or a better job?	❏	❏
Does tobacco make me stronger?	❏	❏	Does tobacco use solve my problems?	❏	❏
Does tobacco improve my appearance?	❏	❏	Does tobacco taste or smell good?	❏	❏
Will my family be proud of my decision to use tobacco?	❏	❏	*Can I come up with one good reason to use tobacco?*	❏	❏

■ **Thinking It Over:** Write **T** for *true* or **F** for *false.*

1. _____ Cigarette smoking is an addictive habit.

2. _____ The percentage of smokers is on the rise.

3. _____ Most smokers say they would like to quit.

4. _____ Most smokers have *not* tried to quit.

5. _____ Smoking can have a bad effect on the senses of smell and taste.

6. _____ Most ex-tobacco users say quitting the habit was an easy thing to do.

■ **Key Vocabulary**

1. When people feel they *must* do something, they are said to have an _____.

2. _____ is a harmful substance found in tobacco.

3. The strength to complete a difficult task is called _____.

■ **Everyday Math**

1. Use information in the reading to figure out what percentage of smokers have *not* tried to quit.

_____

2. After about 16 years of being smoke-free, most human lungs no longer show the bad effects of tobacco use. Carrie stopped smoking when she was 18 years old. At what age should her lungs be like those of a nonsmoker?

_____

■ **Supporting Details:** Read the following statement. Then write three sentences that support the statement.

STATEMENT:

• Tobacco use can be dangerous.

SUPPORT:

• _____

_____

• _____

_____

• _____

_____

■ **On Your Own**

Tell about some of the laws that regulate tobacco use in your region. For example: What is the legal age to purchase tobacco products? What rules apply to smoking in public places? Where is cigarette advertising allowed and where is it banned?

_____

_____

_____

_____

_____

LESSON

3   Alcohol and Illegal Drugs

Ben thought it was cool to drink alcohol. Experimenting with illegal drugs felt wild and exciting. Life in the fast lane, Ben declared, was one big party!

Then Ben discovered the ugly side of alcohol and drugs. He got behind the wheel of a car after drinking. Alcohol made him use bad judgment. It made him drive too fast and slowed his reflexes. Ben crashed his car. Luckily, no one was hurt, but Ben knew that he or someone else might have been killed. A court judge took away Ben's driver's license and sent him to a drug abuse program. Ben says the program saved his life. It forced him to face facts about alcohol and drug use.

Help is available for Ben and others who have problems with alcohol or drug abuse. School counselors, doctors, and social service workers can be useful resources. Information is also available in the yellow pages under "Alcoholism Information and Treatment" or "Drug Abuse Information and Treatment," or online at websites such as http://www.teens.drugabuse.gov.

ALCOHOL FACTS

- Alcohol can kill. Alcohol overdose is the #1 drug-related case seen in hospital emergency rooms. It is the #1 cause of auto accidents.
- Alcohol can harm health. It may interfere with healthy eating and nutrition. It can cause permanent damage to the body.
- Alcohol can ruin innocent lives. Alcohol that a mother drinks during pregnancy can damage her unborn child.
- Alcohol can bring legal trouble. In most places, it is illegal to have alcohol if you're under 21.
- Alcohol can lead to a dangerous illness. Alcoholism is a disease that strikes at any age. Warning signs include drinking to deal with unhappiness, drinking alone or early in the day, missing school or work because of alcohol, needing a drink to "have fun" or "feel at ease," drinking after deciding to stay sober.

DRUG FACTS

Illegal drugs may, in the short term, produce pleasant or exciting feelings. But drugs can produce long-term damage that includes:

- addiction
- money problems
- legal problems

- emotional problems
- family and relationship problems
- work and school problems

- illness
- permanent harm or death

■ **Thinking It Over**

1. Alcohol or drug abuse can cause

    a. long-term damage.

    b. improved reflexes.

    c. better judgment.

2. Alcoholism is a

    a. treatment program.

    b. dangerous disease.

    c. term meaning "drunk driving."

3. According to the reading, the penalty for drunk driving is likely to be

    a. a small fine.

    b. loss of a driver's license.

    c. a stern warning.

4. In most places, the legal age to have alcohol is

    a. 16.   b. 18.   c. 21.

■ **Recalling Details**

1. What is the number one cause of auto accidents?

    _____

2. What is one warning sign of alcoholism?

    _____

    _____

3. According to the reading, at what age is a person most likely to have trouble with alcoholism?

    _____

4. What is one resource people can look to for help with alcohol or drug abuse problems?

    _____

■ **Cause and Effect**

Name three bad effects that drug use can cause.

_____

_____

_____

_____

_____

_____

■ **On Your Own**

1. Write two sentences expressing your views on teen alcohol use.

    _____

    _____

    _____

    _____

2. Explain how each of the following people might encourage a teen to stay drug and alcohol free.

    a. a parent: _____

    _____

    b. a teacher: _____

    _____

    c. a friend: _____

    _____

    d. a store owner: _____

    _____

LESSON

4   Infectious Diseases

Most of us spend our days with other people. That means we live among germs—both viruses and bacteria. Most germs are not harmful, but many germs are infectious. Because germs spread from person to person, we're all likely to catch an illness now and again. Mostly, we come down with short-term ailments like colds and flu. Some infectious diseases, however, are serious health threats. As "social creatures," we need to understand infectious diseases and make efforts to avoid contracting them.

The chart below describes some social activities that may put you at risk for infection. You can stay safe by avoiding high-risk activities or by protecting yourself when engaging in them.

ACTIVITIES: *kissing, sharing food and drinking glasses*

- Infectious mononucleosis is also called *mono* or "the kissing disease." This viral infection begins with a sore throat. Common among teens and young adults, it is usually spread by contact with an infected person's saliva.

- *Strep throat* is a sore throat caused by streptococcal bacteria. Strep is very contagious and easily spread among household members. Strep throat should be treated with antibiotics to avoid complications.

ACTIVITIES: *piercing and tattooing*

- Certain risks come with the use of needles. Think twice before getting a body part pierced or tattooed. If you do, go to a reputable professional who uses brand new, sterile needles. Using an unclean needle, even for a procedure as simple as ear-piercing, can pass on an extremely contagious disease called *hepatitis*. It can also spread the HIV virus* that leads to AIDS**.

  *HIV: Human Immunodeficiency Virus. The virus attacks the immune system, making it hard for your body to fight infections and diseases.

  ** AIDS: Acquired Immune Deficiency Syndrome. This disease is the last stage of HIV. The immune system becomes so weak it can no longer defend against illnesses. Eventually, one of many infections can cause death.

ACTIVITIES: *intimate relationships, sexual intercourse*

- HIV is contracted through contact with an infected person's body fluids. HIV can be spread through sexual intercourse. It is not spread by limited physical contact such as hugging, kissing, or being near someone with the virus.

- STD stands for *Sexually Transmitted Disease*. Because sexual organs are sensitive to bacteria, certain bacterial infections can be spread through intercourse. These diseases are usually curable with antibiotics. Viral STDs, such as herpes and viral hepatitis, can be treated but not cured. In other words, medicine can relieve symptoms but cannot completely get rid of the disease.

■ Thinking It Over

1. An infectious disease is one that is

   a. spread from person to person.

   b. incurable.

   c. painful.

2. Which of the following is *not* a way to contract HIV?

   a. getting a tattoo with an infected needle

   b. having intimate relations with an infected person

   c. shaking hands with an infected person

3. Which of the following activities may put you at risk for a serious infectious disease?

   a. checking a book out of the public library

   b. using a drinking fountain

   c. letting a friend pierce your ears with an old needle

4. The reading suggests it is a good idea to

   a. avoid or be cautious with high-risk activities.

   b. stay away from other people.

   c. avoid antibiotics.

■ Key Vocabulary

1. _____ are medications that fight bacterial infections.

2. An item that is completely clean and germ-free is said to be _____ .

3. A _____ activity involves a chance of danger.

4. The fluid in a person's mouth is called _____ .

■ Recalling Details: Use information from the reading to decide whether each disease is caused by a *virus* or *bacteria*. Write **V** for *virus* or **B** for *bacteria*.

1. _____ mononucleosis

2. _____ strep throat

3. _____ HIV

■ Synonyms: Write a word from the box that has the same meaning as the **boldface** word.

contagious	catch	ailment

1. **sickness** / _____

2. **infectious** / _____

3. **contract** / _____

■ On Your Own

Find out more about an infectious disease mentioned in the reading. Write two facts about the disease.

_____

_____

_____

UNIT [4]

REVIEW | Avoiding Health Hazards

A. Answer the questions to show what you know about the material you studied in this unit.

1. What is one example of a *positive* type of peer pressure?

   _____

2. What is one example of a *negative* type of peer pressure?

   _____

3. What are two ways a person's health is likely to improve if he or she stops using tobacco?

   _____

4. What should you do in the following situations? Make a decision based on what you've read in this unit. Explain your decision.

   • *Your friends are teasing the new girl in class. She looks like she's about to cry.*

   _____

   • *You suspect that your friend has a drinking problem.*

   _____

B. Use key words from the unit to complete the sentences.

1. _____ is an addictive substance found in tobacco.

2. _____ _____ is the number one cause of automobile accidents.

3. _____ is a disease that can cause people to miss work and to need a drink to feel at ease.

4. _____ is an infectious virus that attacks the immune system and can lead to AIDS.

C. How can getting a tattoo be a health risk? Write three explanations.

1. _____
2. _____
3. _____

Abbreviation
ability
abuse
accidents
acids
acne
addiction
aerobic
AIDS (Acquired Immune Deficiency
    Syndrome)
allergies
American Red Cross
anesthetics
annihilate
antacid
antibiotic
antidandruff
antiseptic
appendectomy
appendix
appliances
appointment
arteries
assert

Bacteria
baking soda
balanced diet
bath
behavior
benefit
bleaching

blood pressure
bruises

Calcium
calories
cancer
carbohydrates
cautious
cavity
cereal
chart
check-up
chemicals
childproof
claims
classified
complications
conditions
consciousness
contagious
contract
co-pay
cosmetic
counselor
coverage
creative
cupboards

Dandruff
decay
decongestants
deductible

dentist
depression
dermatologist
diagnosis
diarrhea
diary
diet
directions
discretionary calories
dizzy
document
dosage
drowsiness
DV (Daily Value)

Effective
electricity
emotions
endorphins
energy
enroll
ER (emergency room)
evaluate
examination
exercise
expiration date
expression
extract

Fat
fee-for-services
fever
fiber
fire extinguisher
first aid
fitness
flaky

flames
flexibility
floss
fluids
fluoride
Food Pyramid
forms

General practitioner
generic
germs
grains
grease
guidance
gums

Habit
halitosis
hazard
health care provider
health insurance
heart
hepatitis
herpes
hints
HIV (Human Immune Deficiency Virus)
HMO (Health Maintenance Organization)
hospital
hygiene

Illegal
immune
incurable
infection
ingredient

injure
insure
intercourse
intimate
iodine
iron
itchy

Journal
judgment

Labels
laboratory/lab
landmark
laps
license
lungs

Maintain
managed care
medications
mental health
mole
mononucleosis
mouthwash
mucus
muscles

Needle
negative
nicotine
novocaine
nutrient
nutrition

Oils
ophthalmologist

oral prophylaxis
oral surgeon
organs
orthodontist
orthopedic surgeon
overdose
over-the-counter medicines
oxygen

Pasta
patients
PCP (primary care
    physician)
pediatrician
peer pressure
penalty
percent
peroxide
persists
pharmacist
physical
pimple
plaque
policy
porcelain
portion
positive
poultry
practice
pregnancy
premiums
prescribe/prescription
preventative/prevention
procedures
product
professional
protein

Rash

rate
raw
reactions
recipe
recommend
reduce
referral
region
regulate
reputable
resist
resources
restorative
risk
routines
Rx (prescription)

Saliva

sandwich
scalp
schedule
seizures
session
severe
shampoo
side effects
signal
sober
sodium
specialist
specific
STDs (sexually transmitted diseases)
sterile

strain
strep throat
stress
sunscreens
support
surfaces
surgeon
sweets
symptoms

Tablets

tattoos
technician
tension
therapist
tobacco
toothache
treatment

Units

update
USDA (U.S. Department of Agriculture)
utensils

Vegetables

vegetarian
viruses
vitamin
vocabulary

Wages

workout

Yogurt